The Original
Guitar Case
Scale Book

By Peter Pickow

Exclusive Distributors:
Music Sales Corporation
225 Park Avenue South, New York, NY 10003, USA
Music Sales Limited
8/9 Frith Street, London W1V 5TZ, England
Music Sales Pty. Limited
120 Rothschild Avenue, Rosebery, NSW 2018, Australia

© Copyright 1990 by Amsco Publications
US ISBN 0.8256.2588.2
UK ISBN 0.7119.1906.2
AM 76217

&

Amsco Publications
New York/London/Sydney

*To Amy, who keeps me in mind
of what is possible*

Contents

What Scales Can Do for You

Everybody who plays an instrument knows that practicing scales is important. But many guitarists, especially those of you who are self taught, do not get the benefit that they could from their scales either because they practice without any regularity or organized methodology, or, worse, because they practice scales without fully understanding them. Working with scales can do wonders for your playing, but they are not in and of themselves any kind of shortcut to "superchops." To really get the most out of scale practice, you must understand how different types of scales are constructed, the theory behind those constructions, as well as the best fingerings for different situations. Armed with these tools, an organized program of scale practice can not only provide you with technical facility and fingerboard familiarity, but also with theoretical understanding of tonal and chordal structures and their applications and, consequently, broadened improvising and even composing skills.

The more scales you are truly familiar with, the more choices you have available to you to use in building riffs for a set part or on the spur of the moment in a solo. Your way is also smoother when coming up with more extended melodies or harmony parts if you are confident of your knowledge of scale construction. Even your comping skills are enhanced as you are able to realize new embellishments for standard chords.

How to Use This Book

In the sections that follow, you will find basic explanations of scale theory and application. This material is designed to be general in nature and so it may apply to just about any style of contemporary music. In fact, it is often difficult to generalize about matters of style and genre when discussing musical building blocks as elemental as scales. Just because a scale is categorized as a "jazz" scale for the purposes of this book should not be taken to mean that it never turns up in rock or country or even polka music. On the other hand, if you regularly feature these so-called jazz scales in a more-or-less idiomatic way, your playing will tend to sound more-or-less jazzy.

No matter what your area of musical interest, you should attempt to master and practice all of the scale patterns outlined in the "Scales" section of the book. A few of the scales included are admittedly of limited musical use. Others may seem to have little relevance to the type of music you play. This is no reason to shy away, because practicing these scales may be considered to be technique practice in its purest form. Even if there appears to be little value in a three-octave chromatic or diminished scale, smaller patterns contained within such a scale could crop up in just about any type of musical situation.

If you already have a routine for practicing scales, you may want to use this book simply as a thesaurus of scale forms and practice patterns. Even if you are thoroughly familiar with all of the forms presented, you will find that having all of them together in one source helps you to organize your practice sessions, allowing you to concentrate on the technical and musical aspects of the business at hand.

If you are not already versed in scale practice, pay special attention to the section "How to Practice Scales." Develop your personal routine and stick to it. If you cannot avail yourself of the advice of a good teacher, talk to guitar players you admire; in fact, talk to any guitar players you can. Another good source for ideas and advice is to be found in the many interviews with well-known guitarists, columns, and articles in magazines such as *Guitar Player, Guitar for the Practicing Musician, Guitar World,* and *Frets.* These magazines provide a wealth of supplemental theory and technique material every month in addition to some entertaining features.

Scale Theory

Simply defined, a scale is a series of tones organized according to a specific arrangement of *intervals.* An interval is the distance between any two tones, or pitches. The smallest interval (excepting the *unison*) is the *half step,* which corresponds to the difference in pitch between two notes one fret apart on the same string.

A distance of two half-steps is, naturally, a *whole step.*

Most scales may be defined exclusively by their arrangements of whole and half steps. If you know a scale's formula of whole and half steps, you can construct that scale beginning on any note. For example, examine the layout of the major scale below.

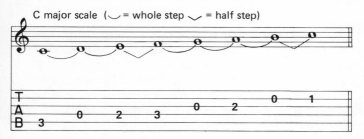

The formula of whole-whole-half-whole-whole-whole-half is the same for any major scale.

Major Scales and Key Signatures

If you look at the C major scale above in two halves, you can see that each half has the same formula of whole and half steps—that is, whole-whole-half—and that the two halves are separated by one whole-step. From what you know about scale formulas, this means that the second half of the C major scale can start off a new major scale. Since this new scale will begin on G, it is said to have a *tonal center* of G, or, more simply, to be a G major scale.

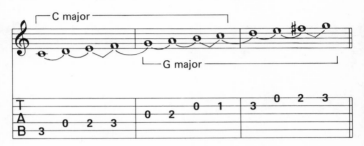

Notice that to keep the arrangement of whole and half steps the same as it was in the C major scale, the seventh degree of the G major scale must be sharped. Since the formula must be consistent, the G major scale will always contain an F-sharp. Because the scale always contains an F-sharp, the *key signature* of the key of G major is written like this:

Let's now take the second half of the G scale and use it as the first half of a new major scale. Notice that we have dropped the G major scale down an octave to put the new scale in a more easily playable range.

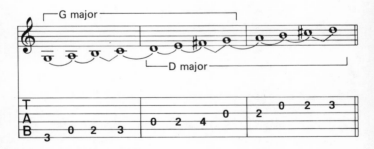

In the same way that the F-sharp was added to the G scale, a C-sharp must be added to the D scale to make it agree with the major-scale formula. This means that the key signature of D major contains two sharps, F and C.

Continuing this process of taking the second half of a major scale to be the first half of the next will produce twelve distinct major scales each with its own distinct key signature. Notice that it is necessary

C

G

D

A

E

B (sounds the same as C-flat)

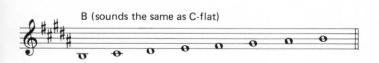

F-sharp (sounds the same as G-flat)

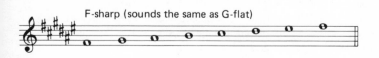

C-sharp (sounds the same as D-flat)

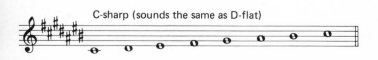

to use flats rather than sharps to produce the scales in the second column of the following chart.

C-flat (sounds the same as B)

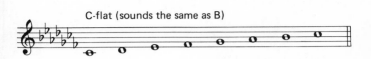

G-flat (sounds the same as F-sharp)

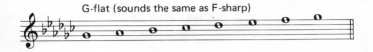

D-flat (sounds the same as C-sharp)

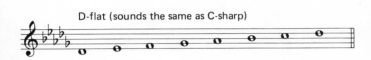

A-flat

E-flat

B-flat

F

C

Although it is not necessary to memorize any of the foregoing material in order to make use of the scales and exercises in this book, having this information at your fingertips—as well as any other music theory you can pick up—can only help your playing.

The Circle of Fifths

The order in which the scales are presented in the chart above is referred to as the *circle of fifths.* It is a circle because it starts and ends at the key of C. It is the circle of fifths because each scale begins on the fifth degree of its preceding scale, or the interval of a perfect fifth above. This relationship of the twelve major scales may be expressed in the following circle diagram.

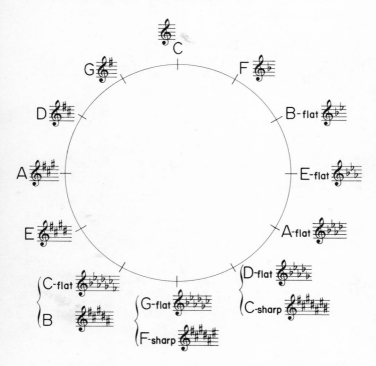

Minor Scales

Every one of the major scales has a corresponding *relative minor* scale that shares the same key signature. You can find the starting note of a major scale's relative minor scale by going up to the sixth degree of that major scale. Thus, the relative minor of C major is A minor.

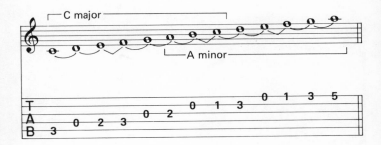

Here is a chart showing all of the relative minor scales.

Major Key	Relative Minor
C Major (no sharps or flats)	A Minor
G Major (one sharp: F♯)	E Minor
D Major (two sharps: F♯, C♯)	B Minor
A Major (three sharps: F♯, C♯, G♯)	F-sharp Minor
E Major (four sharps: F♯, C♯, G♯, D♯)	C-sharp Minor
B Major (five sharps: F♯, C♯, G♯, D♯, A♯)	G-sharp Minor
F-sharp Major (six sharps: F♯, C♯, G♯, D♯, A♯, E♯)	D-sharp Minor
C-sharp Major (seven sharps: F♯, C♯, G♯, D♯, A♯, E♯, B♯)	A-sharp Minor
F Major (one flat: B♭)	D Minor
B-flat Major (two flats: B♭, E♭)	G Minor
E-flat Major (three flats: B♭, E♭, A♭)	C Minor
A-flat Major (four flats: B♭, E♭, A♭, D♭)	F Minor
D-flat Major (five flats: B♭, E♭, A♭, D♭, G♭)	B-flat Minor
G-flat Major (six flats: B♭, E♭, A♭, D♭, G♭, C♭)	E-flat Minor
C-flat Major (seven flats: B♭, E♭, A♭, D♭, G♭, C♭, F♭)	A-flat Minor

Harmonic and Melodic Minor Scales

The relative minor scales referred to above are known as *natural minor* scales because they occur naturally, without deviating from their key signatures. These scales are commonly altered to form *harmonic minor* and *melodic minor* scales. The harmonic minor scale is formed by raising the seventh degree of a natural minor.

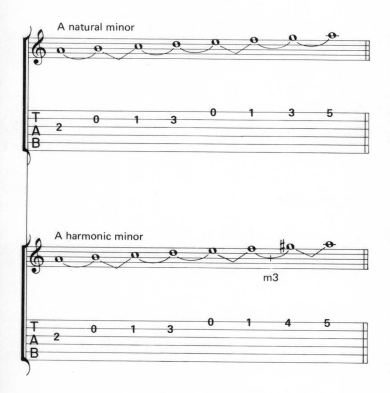

Notice that the interval formula for a harmonic minor scale includes one interval that is neither a whole step nor a half step. The *minor third*, abbreviated *m3*, is equal to three half-steps.

The other common type of minor scale is the *melodic minor* scale, produced by raising the sixth and seventh degrees of the natural minor scale.

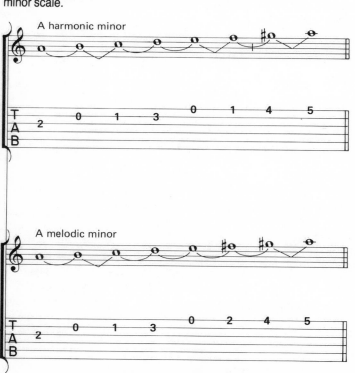

Notice that the second half of the interval formula of a melodic minor scale is identical to that of a major scale. In fact, the only difference between a melodic minor scale and a major scale is the third degree.

Traditionally, the melodic minor scale form is said to follow the formula of the natural minor when descending.

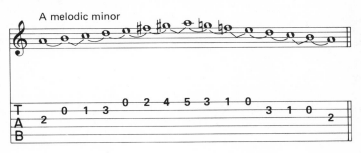

In recent times, it has become theoretically preferable to retain the same formula descending as ascending. Most people who think of the melodic minor in this way refer to it as a *jazz melodic minor* to distinguish it from the traditional interpretation. You will only find forms for the traditional melodic minor presented in the pages that follow, but you may easily practice jazz melodic minors by simply applying the same fingering going down as you do going up.

Modes

Modes are produced by displacing the starting point of a scale without changing its interval formula. This has the effect of turning out a scale with a new arrangement of whole and half steps. Most often, when musicians talk about modes they are referring to the seven modes of the major scale, although modes may be generated from any scale at all.

The modes are known by their Greek names (which were given to them by some rather creative Medieval theoreticians and have very little to do with Greece or Greek music).

The Dorian Mode

Starting on the second degree of a major scale yields a *Dorian* scale. This scale is very useful in jazz and jazz/rock—in which it is used for soloing over minor seventh chords—and sounds like the natural minor with a raised sixth.

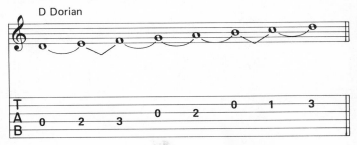

The Phrygian Mode

Playing a C major from E to E gives us an E *Phrygian* scale; reminiscent of flamenco music and sounding like the natural minor with a flatted second.

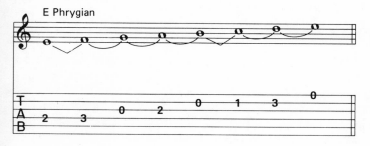

The Lydian Mode

The mode starting on the fourth degree of the major scale is known as a *Lydian* scale. This one has a major sound but differs from a straight major scale in its sharped fourth. In jazz, Lydian mode scales are generally used for soloing over major seventh chords other than the I chord.

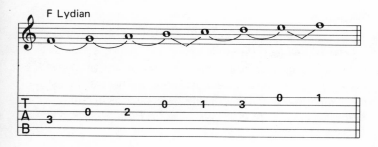

The Mixolydian Mode

Starting on the fifth degree of a major scale produces another major-sounding scale, the *Mixolydian* mode; this time with a flatted seventh. You will hear this one a lot in folk and rock music.

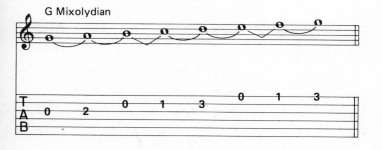

The Aeolian Mode

Remember that starting on the sixth degree of a major scale produces its relative minor. In the terminology of the modes, major is called *Ionian* and natural minor, *Aeolian*.

The Locrian Mode

The seventh mode, *Locrian,* was avoided for centuries due to its truly weird flavor. Because the scale outlines a diminished chord, melodies written in the Locrian mode never seem to quite come to rest. Inasmuch as this is sometimes a desirable quality in modern music, this mode has come into its own during the twentieth century. Also, the Locrian is useful in jazz soloing where it is commonly used over minor seventh flat-five (half-diminished) chords.

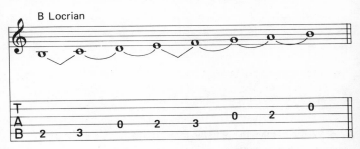

Chromatic Scales

A *chromatic* scale is the simplest example of a type of scale known as a *symmetrical* scale. The formula for a chromatic scale is simply all half steps.

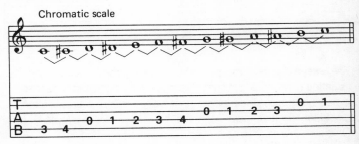

Because the intervals between notes are all identical, any note in the scale may be considered its root: no matter where you start, the formula will come out the same.

The chromatic scale is not really used as a scale for improvising (unless you consider that every melody is made up of notes from the chromatic scale—but that is not a very useful point of view). Since every type of music uses chromatic passages from time to time, the various patterns for this scale are well worth practicing.

Rock Scales

Major Pentatonic Scales

In addition to the usual major, minor, and modal scales, much rock music is based on five-note scales called *pentatonic* scales. The basic form of pentatonic scale is the major pentatonic built from the first, second, third, fifth, and sixth degrees of a major scale. This scale is often heard in Southern rock, rhythm and blues, country music, and light rock.

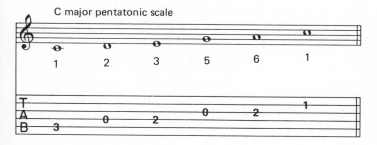
C major pentatonic scale

Minor Pentatonic, or Blues, Scales

By taking the relative minor of the major pentatonic scale, you can produce a *minor pentatonic,* or *blues,* scale. Thus the C major pentatonic above becomes an A blues scale by starting it on A.

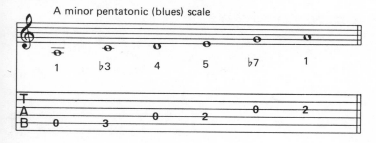
A minor pentatonic (blues) scale

The reason that the minor pentatonic scale is good for blues lies in its flatted third—flatted in comparison to the third of the major scale. In blues—and, consequently in most rock—the third degree is often ambiguous; neither major nor minor, but somewhere in between. On guitar, this effect is easy to produce with string bending.

In addition to the ambiguous "blue" third, the pentatonic blues scale is commonly ornamented by adding the normal major third and the flatted fifth.

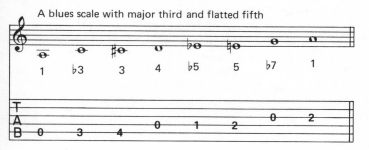
A blues scale with major third and flatted fifth

Besides being used in traditional and progressive blues, the pentatonic blues scale is commonly found in heavy metal music and all
other types of rock, as well as some types of jazz.

Jazz Scales

There are many theories concerning the application of scales to
jazz improvisation—some say there are as many theories as there
are jazz players. The brief descriptions of how the following scales
are commonly used should not therefore be taken as gospel, but
rather as springboards to your further investigation of jazz theory.

Jazz Melodic Minor

As stated above, a *jazz melodic minor* scale is nothing more than a
traditional melodic minor scale with the same formula descending
as ascending (see "Minor Scales" above). The jazz melodic minor
scale may be used to generate the *Lydian flat-seven* scale (see
below).

Lydian Flat-Seven Scales

The *Lydian flat-seven* scale is generally used for soloing over dominant seventh chords other than the V chord of the progression (for
which the Mixolydian scale usually suffices). The formula of the
scale reveals it to be a cross between a Mixolydian and a Lydian
scale, containing a flatted seventh and a sharped fourth (as com-
pared to a major scale). This scale may also be thought of as the
Lydian mode of the jazz melodic minor.

Diminished Scales

Like the chromatic scale, the *diminished* scale is a symmetrical scale, in that more than one note in the scale may be considered the root. Since its formula is a repeating alternation of whole-step/half-step, starting on every other degree will yield three other scales with identical formulas. Because of this, the C diminished scale shown below could also be considered an E-flat diminished scale, a G-flat diminished scale, or an A diminished scale.

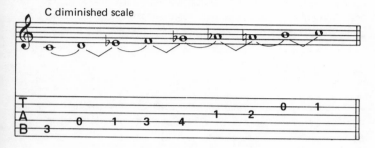

In addition to being used to solo over diminished seventh chords, the diminished scale is often used over dominant seventh chords to add tensions (flat-nine, sharp-nine, sharp-eleven, and thirteen). When used in this way, the root of the diminished scale should be one half-step above the root of the seventh chord.

Whole-Tone Scales

Another symmetrical scale is the *whole-tone* scale. Where the formula of the chromatic scale comprises all half steps and that of the diminished scale consists of alternating whole and half steps, all intervals in the whole-tone scale are whole steps.

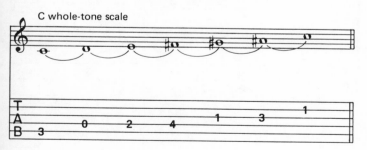

This scale goes well with augmented seventh chords because it contains all the tones of the chord plus the ninth and the sharped eleventh.

Altered Scales

Combining the first half of the diminished scale with the second half of the whole-tone scale (one half-step above) yields the *altered* scale, used against dominant seventh chords altered with the tensions flat-five, sharp-five, flat-nine, sharp-nine, and/or sharp-eleven.

Notice that the formula of the diminished-scale portion of the C altered scale above shows it to be based on a D-flat diminished scale, even though it starts on C, a half step below. Notice also that while the diminished scale has eight steps per octave and the whole-tone scale only six, the altered scale has seven steps per octave just like the standard major, minor, and modal scales.

How to Practice Scales

Practicing scales is a perfect form of musical exercise: It combines dexterity and two-hand coordination exercise with development of velocity, strength, and endurance. In addition, there is valuable ear training and rhythmic discipline to be gained. All of these benefits come to you more or less automatically when you practice regularly and correctly. The good news is that there is no one correct way to practice and that the best method for you is one that you develop for yourself. The key is to get organized and stick to your organization. As you know by now, when it comes to your playing, you will always be your own most severe critic. Use these critical faculties to help you stay on the right track.

Here are some suggestions—some specific, some general—that will help you develop your personal regimen. Pay careful attention to all them—in fact, be sure to apply each one of them sooner or later.

• If you practice an hour a day, ten to fifteen minutes should be spent on scales. Adjust this time period up or down proportionately to the total time you practice each day.

• Start out each session with something easy and familiar to you— say, a one-octave major-scale pattern moved chromatically (fret by fret) up and down the fingerboard.

• Sing every scale as you play it. This is especially beneficial when learning new fingering patterns for familiar-sounding scales as it aids your sense of ear-hand coordination. This is the skill that enables accomplished improvisers to spontaneously play any melodic ideas that they can imagine.

• Alternate playing mechanically and musically. Try variations of phrasing and articulation ranging from robotic staccato to expressive, flowing legato.

• Use a metronome or drum machine. Good sense of tempo and rhythm is essential to all music. A metronome will help you keep track of your progress as you increase speed. Remember, never practice anything faster than you can play it well.

• Try using the metronome (or drum machine) to give you the tempo, then turn it off and play a scale or scale exercise. As you finish, turn the metronome back on and see if you ended at the same tempo as you started. (This is a killer at extremely slow tempos—try it!)

• Play cross-rhythms against a drum machine. For example, play a triplet pattern while the drum machine plays a straight eighth-note pattern so that you are playing three against two. Or play straight eighth notes to the drum machine's shuffle pattern so that you are playing two against three.

• Play familiar patterns backwards or from different starting points. We tend to think of scales as going up then down. To add variety, start at the top and go down then up. If you want to find out how well you really know a particular fingering pattern, start it somewhere in the middle.

• Use scales to learn new right-hand techniques. If you play primarily with a pick, explore the fingerstyle patterns given below, or vice versa. Choose familiar scale patterns, for which the left-hand part is totally automatic.

Practice Patterns for All Scales

The practice patterns given below fall into two general categories: patterns for ordering tones within a scale and patterns for ordering the scales themselves. Using the different suggestions, or any patterns that you come up with, in various combinations can help to keep scale practice interesting and challenging.

Since it is in the nature of these patterns to be repetitive, some of them are written out in somewhat abbreviated forms. In all cases, though, you will find enough to give you the idea.

Patterns for Ordering Scale Tones

The following ideas for practice patterns have been developed with several goals in mind: Some of them are designed to be easy to learn and remember, making them excellent choices for quick warm-ups. Others will take some time to understand and master, making them better at providing more in-depth exploration of the fingerboard. After looking these patterns over, you will no doubt see how easy it is to come up with your own variations or original ideas. The trick is to try to inject some musicality into what is essentially a mathematical sequence.

All of the following examples are based on this simple C major scale pattern.

Be sure to apply them to any other major and minor scale patterns you know or are trying to learn. Most of them may be adapted to chromatic, diminished, whole-tone, and altered scales as well.

Eighth-Note Patterns

These patterns are all written out in straight eighth notes. You may play them as written, or impose a different rhythm or accent pattern on them. For example, you might choose to play the patterns in "swing eighth notes":

Or you could dictate a rhythmic pattern such as the following, which is reminiscent of a Scottish hornpipe.

As far as your right hand goes, use any or all of the pick and finger-style patterns suggested below—or come up with your own patterns based on movements that you are trying to master.

Pick-Style Alternation Patterns

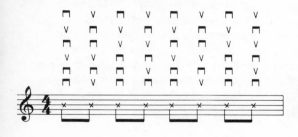

⊓ = downstroke

V = upstroke

Fingerstyle Alternation Patterns

i = index finger

m = middle finger

a = ring finger

Here are a few ideas derived from various interval skips.

The following patterns employ repeated motifs—try using hammerons and pulloffs (indicated by slurs in the examples) wherever possible to build strength.

Outlining the chords contained within a scale is good ear-training practice. Watch out for the way that these patterns reverse at the top.

Triplet Patterns

Patterns based on triplet rhythms force you to deal with a whole other set of accent figures. You can use the same right-hand alternation patterns given above for the eighth-note patterns, and, in addition, you may want to apply some of these.

Pick-Style Alternation Patterns

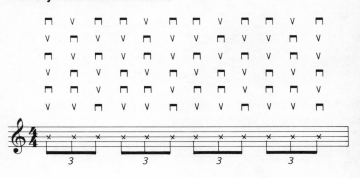

Fingerstyle Alternation Patterns

You can impose rhythmic variations on the triplet patterns in the same way as was outlined above for the eighth-note patterns. Here are a couple of variations you might try.

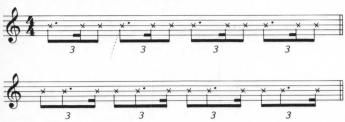

A good way to get into triplet patterns is simply to play a scale in triplets. Remember to try all of the different alternation patterns. (In the following example, notice how the in-position C major scale has been expanded to its upper and lower limits.)

The following employ various techniques of repetition and interval skips to produce useful practice patterns.

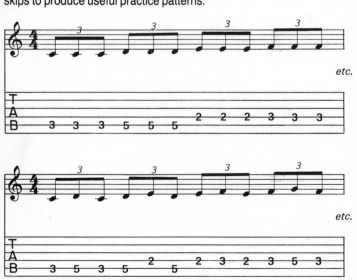

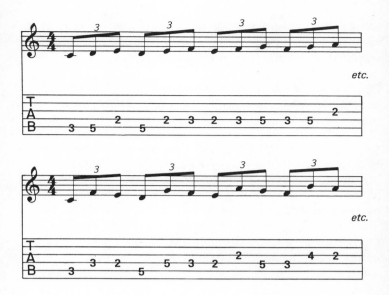

A Melodic Alternative

Probably the most musical way to generate practice patterns is to simply play a simple diatonic melody or melodic fragment starting on each note of the scale. You could also play the tune using different scale forms. In fact, playing the same melody out of several different scale patterns is a good way to get familiar with the melody as well as with the scale pattern. Here is an example using a Charlie Parker riff which stays within a major scale.

Patterns for Ordering Scales

The two categories of patterns for ordering scales are those that provide an order for a single scale fingering and those that provide an order for a series of scales. The simplest configuration of the former category is to move a scale form up and down by half steps; that is, one fret at a time. Starting in fifth or seventh position can add some variety and make a new fingering easier to learn.

Other good patterns for this type of practice would consist of interval skips such as going up by whole steps or going up a whole step and down a half step.

To practice different scale forms, the easiest order to use is that of the circle of fifths. Try this with any one quality of scale—major, diminished, pentatonic, etc. Pick the appropriate form and starting point for each scale to give you a pattern that stays close to one position or one that jumps around a lot.

Classical guitarists have long practiced major scales and their relative melodic minor scales around the circle of fifths in this pattern.

C	A minor
G	E minor
D	B minor
A	F-sharp minor
E	C-sharp minor
B	G-sharp minor
F-sharp	D-sharp minor
D-flat	B-flat minor
A-flat	F minor
E-flat	C minor
B-flat	G minor
F	D minor

This is an excellent way to make sure that you hit every key.

The Scales

In-Position Major Scales

These scales are remarkably versatile tools. They give you seven
starting points for basic major scales within one position on the
neck. They are all moveable forms (containing no open strings), and
each one covers a little over two octaves. If you really have a command of these forms, you will find that you can play any major (or
modal) scale within one fret of any position you may be in. Note that
although each of these stays within one four-fret position, some of
them contain stretches up with the fourth finger or down with the first
finger. These stretches are indicated by the letter *s*.

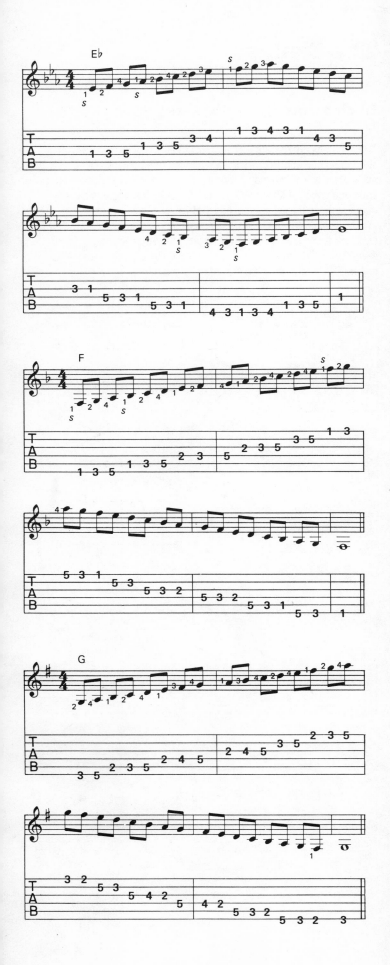

Here's an idea for practicing these scales that will really get them under your fingers: Play each scale form starting from the same root. For example, if you were to start from G-flat, the C scale form would be moved to eighth position, the D scale form to sixth position, the E-flat to fifth position, and so on. This would give you the G-flat scale in all seven positions.

In-Position Minor Scales

Any of the major-scale forms above may be transformed into a natural minor scale by simply starting on the sixth degree; thus C major becomes A natural minor, D major becomes B minor, E-flat major becomes C minor, and so on. Since the harmonic and melodic minor scale forms require different fingerings, they are written out below.

Harmonic Minor Scales

To produce harmonic minor scales, you simply sharp the seventh degree.

D harmonic minor

E harmonic minor

Melodic Minor Scales

Remember that there are two kinds of melodic minor scales and that the forms in this book are of the "traditional" variety. If you want to practice jazz melodic minor scales, use the same fingering descending as ascending.

A melodic minor

B melodic minor

C melodic minor

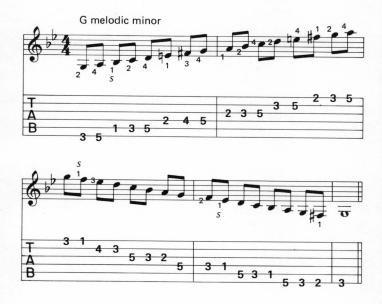

G melodic minor

Chromatic Scales

Since the chromatic scale has no real tonal center, there is no need to present forms with different starting points. The following two forms differ only in fingering.

Chromatic

Chromatic

Rock Scales

You can derive pentatonic scales from any major or minor scale by just taking the appropriate five tones and leaving out the rest (as outlined above in the "Scale Theory" section). The following are the most often used forms of these scales.

Major Pentatonic Scales

C major pentatonic
(with position shifts)

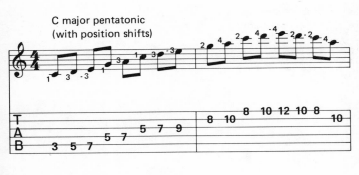

Minor Pentatonic Scales

G minor pentatonic
(in - position)

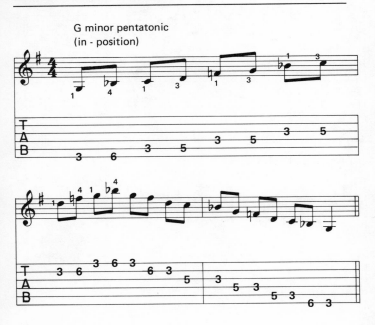

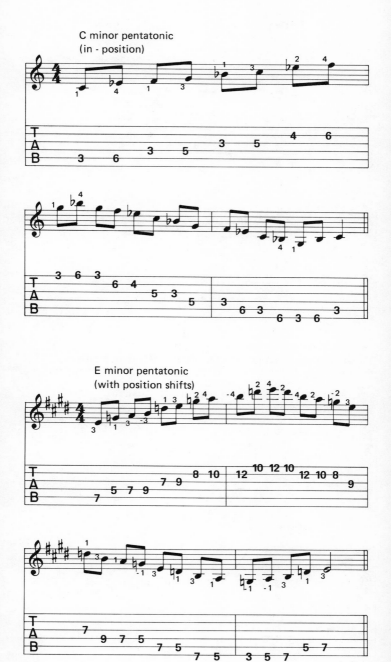

C minor pentatonic
(in - position)

E minor pentatonic
(with position shifts)

A minor pentatonic
(with position shifts)

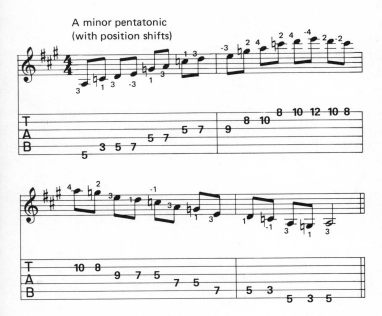

Blues Scales with Major Third and Flatted Fifth

G blues scale with major third and flatted fifth
(in - position)

C blues scale with major third and flatted fifth
(in - position)

E blues scale with major third and flatted fifth
(with position shifts)

A blues scale with major third and flatted fifth
(with position shifts)

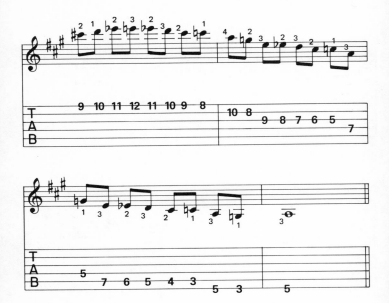

Jazz Scales

Since the jazz melodic minor scale is so similar to the traditional melodic minor, it is not necessary to detail any new forms for it. Let's take a look at the Lydian mode of the jazz melodic minor, known as the Lydian flat-seven.

Lydian Flat-Seven Scales

Compare these in-position forms to the melodic minor forms given above to understand their modal connection.

C Lydian flat-seven

Diminished Scales

Here are two common in-position fingerings and one "sliding scale" fingering for the diminished scale. Remember that every other note may be considered the root, so practice these forms with different starting points to learn them thoroughly.

C, E♭, G♭, or A diminished

G, B♭, C♯, or E diminished

Whole-Tone Scales

Since the whole-tone scale has a perfectly symmetrical formula,
what was said about the diminished scales above goes double
here: Practice these forms considering each and every scale tone
as the root.

Altered Scales

Here are four good in-position patterns for altered scales.

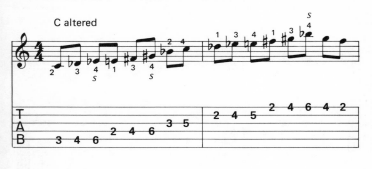

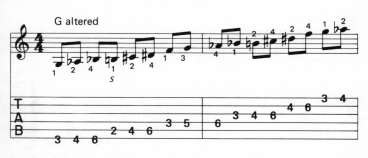

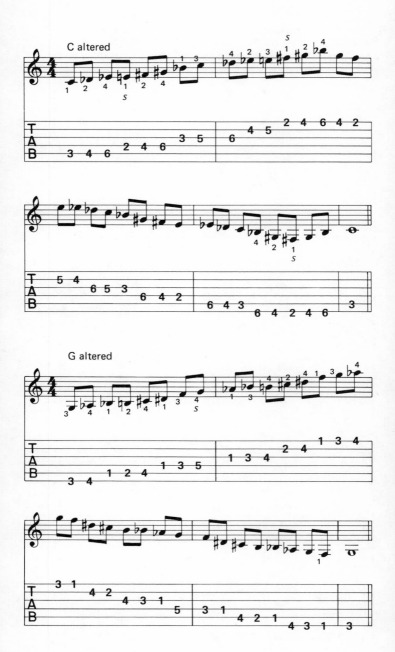

Ideas for Extended Scales

If one of the reasons that you practice scales is to help you learn the fingerboard, then developing fingerings for *extended,* or *up-and-across,* scales should be one of your priorities. The idea behind this type of scale pattern is to start on the lowest note on your instrument that is part of the scale and play the scale through to the highest note on the instrument that is part of the scale. The better your understanding of the scale's formula, the easier it will be to come up with a workable fingering for an extended version of that scale.

Following are three examples of up-and-across fingerings; one each for a major, a melodic minor, and an altered scale. After mastering these, try creating your own by following the guidelines below.

F altered (extended)

As you may have deduced from studying the above patterns, the rules for creating up-and-across fingering patterns are rather loose. The idea is to space out the notes of the scale across the entire fingerboard, avoiding a concentration in any one position. The general rules are to start on low E or F, then use a fingering pattern similar to one of the ones in the scales above. After playing four to six notes of the scale on the sixth string, move *across* to the fifth string and find the next note of the scale with your first finger. Then, slide *up* one or two frets to find the next note of the scale on the fifth string. At this point you can use any fingering pattern that will allow you to play the next three or four notes in the scale. Repeat this procedure, always sliding *up* every time you move *across,* until you reach the absolute highest note in the scale possible on the guitar.

Coming back down, reverse the process so that you are always sliding *down* to find the next lowest note in the scale with your fourth finger each time you move *across* to the next lowest string. Notice that you will always have to derive a descending pattern different from the ascending one in an extended-scale fingering pattern.

There will be many variations on these fingering patterns that you will be able to discover, and it is positively valuable to practice different up-and-across patterns for the same scale.

I hope that the scales and concepts presented in this little volume will help you to reach a better understanding of scale construction, theory, and usage. I know that you will see and feel a tremendous improvement in your playing and in your command of the fretboard if you apply these ideas, many of which are just the starting points for further study or practice. There are many excellent sources available that will allow you to learn more scales and how the different types of scales may be applied in improvisation and composition. For now, good luck—and keep practicing and playing.